KEYS TO BETTER RESOLUTION:
Simple tips on How to attract anyone.

James M. Fain

Table of contents

Chapter 1

Truth about conversation

When most of us converse, we do not genuinely listen to what the other person is saying. This entails focusing on ourselves rather than the person we communicate with. We are constantly working to improve our side of the conversation.

We do not engage in discourse when we approach a conversation with our fully formed side. We're performing a screenplay. A genuine dialogue involves a certain level of uncertainty. We are concerned because of the delay. We still don't know what the other person will say.

Waiting for someone to think things through before speaking can be awkward.
That isn't to imply it shouldn't be done. There is no room for pre-programmed reactions, and we must be sensitive to what

the other person says. Actual conversation necessitates ignorance.

Pay close attention. When speaking with someone, turn your attention away from what you want to say and toward what the other person is saying. Please pay attention to what and how it is being said. To clarify any ambiguities, ask questions. Investigate the speaker's emotional state gently; if you believe she is upset or angry, ask her to express it verbally:

"You're speaking calmly, but I understand you're upset." "Are you sure?" Collect as much relevant information from the speaker as you can, and then, when it's your turn to speak, don't.

For a moment, consider what you've previously heard. Breathe from the belly to allow the words to sink in. Remind yourself that you are connected to this person and all life and that what you say might have far-reaching implications that you are unaware of. Allow yourself to touch on the Ayin level of reliance on the other person. Start by looking the other person in the eyes and saying.

How to Handle Crucial Conversations
Have you ever spoken something and realized you'd regret it as soon as you said it? Ouch. Unfortunately, this frequently occurs when we discuss a highly important or sensitive matter, are stressed or pressed for time, and are in the presence of significant people.

Following character development, good communication is one of the most crucial skill sets for a leader to develop. Indeed, empathy is the foundation of all excellent communication and is required for character development.

While learning to communicate as a leader regularly is essential, knowing how to communicate during a critical conversation is critical. People will forgive a faux pas when the stakes are low, but when the stakes are high, egos are on high alert, and emotions are strong, they will find it inexcusable. Great leaders must tread carefully and wisely at these times.

While crucial or critical talks take up only a tiny percentage of our conversational time, they tremendously impact our relationships with others.

A discussion with an employee about poor performance, demotion, or rejection of an opportunity, for example, a meeting with a spouse about significant parenting problems or a conversation with a business partner or coworker about a work-related issue. A high level of importance, risk, and vulnerability on both sides usually mark these interactions. These crucial conversations can make or break a leader's reputation, influencing whether it soars to great heights or flounders in mediocrity.

Learning to handle challenging conversations can help you build cooperative and rewarding relationships, trust, and confidence with the people who matter most to you while growing your leadership muscles. Take a look at the following:

Begin with the facts. It is always easier to be compassionate and sincere when you talk openly and honestly. Others may not like hearing it, but they will appreciate and respect your sincerity.

Be sincere. Try not to be someone other than yourself. Speak from the heart, using your own words and style and demonstrating courage and honesty.

Gather your thoughts. Consider what you want to say and how you want to convey it. Allow yourself plenty of time. Take a deep breath and slow down if your emotions are running high. Never give up the reins. While it may seem like a lifetime to you, the pause in the conversation is natural and healthy.

Get some distance. Consider the dialogue from the perspective of the other person. Consider the issue from the other person's perspective and try to understand their emotional state. We develop tunnel vision when we are on high alert and determined to finish our script.

Full stops should be avoided. Avoid using emotionally charged words or phrases that can erupt and bring the discourse to a halt. Avoid using phrases like "you should," "always," or highly offensive terms. Speak in the manner in which you like to be addressed.

Keep it short. You can avoid a long buildup by getting to the point early in the conversation. Your crucial point should have been conveyed within the first minute, if not within the first 30 seconds.

Concentrate on the issue rather than the person. Leaders build people up based on their strengths rather than weaknesses and do so verbally. They concentrate on the topic at hand rather than the individual.

Say more with less talking. Prioritize the quality of the conversation over the quantity. Say what needs to be said, then move on. Prevent the conversation from devolving into a lengthy session that will generate ancillary issues and create new problems in the future.

Bring up only a few issues at a time. Deal with one problem at a time to avoid an argument becoming overly complex and out of hand. Avoid attempting to solve multiple problems at the same time. Do not focus on your performance, regardless of what happens or how you believe you performed.

Other themes will be discussed at a later date.

Self-doubt erodes confidence and reduces future effectiveness. Allow it to stand once you've given it your all! Handle the conversation as best you can before moving on.

A brief examination of truth number one: What is truth?

"What is truth?" you wonder.

I enjoy it when you ask those big questions that make you wonder about everything that set you back as you try to figure out what the question even means, let alone whether you can provide an answer...

What is the definition of truth?

It's a tricky question in our Age of Lies1.

I'll provide a detailed and extensive response.

...Or maybe not.

It's not that I'm angry.

I wouldn't say I like using three words when one would do.

So here goes:

Reality is vital to the truth.

I saw you scratching your chin.

"That's all there is to it?"

That's the end of it.

2: Venn

If you draw a Venn diagram to represent the link between truth and reality, one circle,

TRUTH, will completely encircle another, REALITY.
When a claim or assertion departs from reality, it no longer holds.

It exits both of these Venn diagrams.
3. Realism

"But what exactly is reality?" you wonder. "You've simply sidestepped the issue of truth by shifting the burden of explanation back a little."

I get what you're saying. It's the equivalent of responding to "God" in response to the question, "Where did the universe come from?"

It is not a solution but rather a postponement. This raises the following question... "Where did God come from?"

So, what is reality exactly?

I've already answered that question, but I'll try again.
The reality is as follows:

It's the genuine article, the stuff of the universe, the real world.

It is objective, consistent, unique, and self-contained2.

This is not your fault. Whether you like it or not, it exists.
It can be quantified, researched, discovered, and verified.

To put it bluntly, what is reality? Everything is genuine.

Is it enough for you?

4: Logic

Furthermore, the relationship between reality and truth is simple to understand.

Here's how it works:

A mistake

You are mistaken if you believe something
and claim it to be accurate, but it contradicts
reality.
A lie

You're lying if you recognize something
contradicts reality yet insist it's the truth.

Truth
If you believe in anything that mirrors the
real world to the best of our collective
human understanding, you have the truth.3

5: Words

Other qualities of truth are comparable to
those of reality.

Truth is consistent, logical, and objective. Truth can never be contradicted. When you accept 'truths' contradicting each other, you talk about something different than reality. You're referring to ideas, beliefs, plots, or points of view.

The truth is not a personal opinion.

There are no such things as my truth' and 'your truth.'

If you think there is, you've misread the meaning of the word "truth." You used the words 'beliefless' and 'believing' interchangeably.

Why use the word 'truth' when discussing 'belief'?
Sixth: Categories

Some claim that truth is 'just a word,' entangled in a web of words from which it can never escape.

This, however, is known as a category error. Language, symbols, and images all fall into the same category, which we'll call the "depictive category."

However, the objects displayed are not mine.

Words convey information. That is their intention. That is why we hire them. We didn't begin grunting to complain about grunts. Our grunts started as approval, alarm, warning, and excitement.

Then we advanced a little further.

You can say that 'death' is just a word, but try being dead. It's entirely different.

7. Points of view

Is everyone free to express themselves?

We certainly are; there is no doubt about it.

However, being free to believe in something does not make it accurate.

Furthermore, specific points of view are more sincere than others.

The more valuable and applicable an idea, theory, or point of view is, the closer it is to the truth.

The dentist is ranked eighth.

Your egalitarian tendencies compel you to take action. "But, surely, one person's opinion is just as valid as another's, no matter what?"

I've heard that assertion before, but it's usually from folks who want us to believe something absurd or wrong.
Is my opinion of your dental health as trustworthy as your dentist's?

Nope, it doesn't.

I still need to train or study to gain that information.

Please do not allow me to go too close to your teeth.

9: Expertise in your field
"Ah!" you shout, thinking this is your chance to catch me off guard. "But what about two dentists with opposing viewpoints?" "So, what happens now?"

So, allow me to pose a question to you. What is your personal choice between the two options?
You'd think you'd want the most experienced dentist to drill between your teeth. The one with a successful track record? Who knows the most about teeth,

jaws, and gums and whose opinion is more solidly based on facts?
Which dentist would I prefer to see?

10. Independence
This helps to explain why we have theories, points of view, and opinions. Do they have any value? Why should you use or accept them?

Theories, ideas, points of view, and beliefs have value because they are relevant to and close to reality. Their worth is judged by how much they explain and how much help they can provide. The more closely an idea, concept, theory, or point of view resembles reality - the closer it is to being true - the more legitimate it becomes.

Reality and truth strengthen us, whereas lies, deception, and misbelief deprive us of power.

That is why power-hungry people frequently lie. If they know the truth, they have an advantage over us.
Because of this, the truth is always valuable.

It provides us with an advantage.

11: Self-defense

Finally, here are some definitions:

Reality is the state of affairs as they currently exist.

Facts are claims about reality that can be proven or verified.

What is proper and relates to fact or reality is what is true.

Authoritarians and despots employ ambiguity regarding the facts to their advantage. Those who want to influence or

fool us will continuously call into doubt the
value of reality.

Chapter 2

Easy ways to get over your fear about the approach
.

Tips for Overcoming Fear and Anxiety
Conscious attitudes
Anxiety and Fear can have an impact on your life. You can overcome them by following these helpful suggestions.

Anxiety entails focusing on the future rather than the present risk. Your body's reaction to Fear warns you of a possible threat. Everyone has similar experiences from time to time, so understanding how to cope with Fear and dread can be beneficial.

Everyone sometimes feels apprehension and concern, but when these feelings linger, they can be dangerous. It may occasionally prevent you from appreciating the present moment and grasping new chances. Your life may be interrupted, and your mental health may suffer. When a situation becomes paralyzing and causes avoidance, it may be time to learn how to deal with Fear and concern. While you may want to avoid things that make you nervous, avoiding potential stressors will prevent you from developing and enjoying life.

By confronting your fears, you may keep control of your life and avoid letting anxiety rule it. You may learn how to conquer worry and fear on your terms.

7 Ways to Overcome Anxiety and Fear
Fear and concern may have an impact on your life and well-being. Overcoming Fear and anxiety can help you live a more purposeful and happier life.

1. Recognize and comprehend your Fear.
Understanding Fear and anxiety is essential before conquering them. Understanding your Fear will assist you in understanding why it exists and how to overcome it.

Writing down your emotions, concerns, and fears in a journal might help you learn more. When you study the root of your Fear, you may uncover something previously unknown, such as your procedures for dealing with the situation. Writing will help you process the problem and think more clearly in the future.

2. Visualize a successful outcome.
We sometimes forget that we have control over our feelings and thoughts when experiencing dread and worry, but we do.

Using your imagination to see yourself effectively dealing with a difficult situation is a good idea. When Fear or anxiety prompts you to imagine the worst-case scenario, you can actively transition to a pleasurable experience. If you're apprehensive about a job interview, imagine the ideal setting where you instantly connect with the interviewer and demonstrate your best attributes.

3. Practice mindful meditation
When you feel Fear or concern, spend some peaceful time with your emotions. Sit quietly, center yourself in the present moment, and do nothing else.

Mindfulness meditation has been shown to improve emotional control and self-acceptance. As you practice mindfulness, take note of your current feelings. Allow yourself to experience any negative emotions. Allow the emotion to wash over you, and then let it go.

You may recognize that while these feelings are unpleasant, they are controllable. This can help to make your worries and fears appear less overwhelming and controlling. It can also act as a reminder that these feelings are transitory.

4. Enjoy the outdoors
According to a 2019 study, spending time in nature enhances your well-being and strengthens your resilience. You can accept new experiences and opportunities by overcoming Fear and worry.

A 2018 study found that exercising outside can help to quiet your mind, increase your mood, and develop a positive mindset.
Being outside also provides health benefits, such as: Heart rate control blood pressure reduction
Relaxing the muscles reduces the creation of stress chemicals.

5. Keep doing things.
If you are suffering from Fear or anxiety, you may want to avoid circumstances, locations, social interactions, etc. The only way to conquer Fear is to confront it and take action.

Do your most challenging thing to overcome your worries, even if it means starting small. It can be done in small doses, halting if it becomes too difficult. Continue to try and tackle your fears until you are at ease.

6. Use deep breathing exercises.
Deep breathing allows you to focus your thoughts and let rid of negativity. When you are anxious, you may take short breaths, which might lead to a panic attack.

Using breathing techniques, you can avoid the experience and get through it. You may relax and de-stress as you face your Fear by controlling your breathing.

7. Make use of visuals
When something frightens you, visualize yourself triumphantly overcoming it. Consider completing the work that is causing you to worry. You'll feel more secure about going on and overcoming obstacles if you visualize it.

Another possibility is guided visualization, a mindfulness method that uses your imagination to enhance self-control, motivation, and other positive emotions. Combating anxiety and Fear with attentive behaviors

Although dealing with Fear and anxiety can be difficult, you can conquer them and move on. A mindful mentality can assist you in letting go of Fear and living your life.

Mindfulness decreases stress and improves coping, so shifting your perspective may make regulating your emotions more manageable.

Fear and worry should be recognized for what they are.
When your thoughts turn negative, shift your attitude to acceptance rather than judgment. If you accept your experience and learn to sit with the anguish of dread and

worry, you may see that you can withstand more than you believe and that the discomfort will eventually fade.

This acceptance might also assist you in approaching the problem from a different perspective. Consider an alternative point of view to challenge your beliefs while accepting your emotions.

Look for the bright side.
Things may not always go as planned, causing Fear and anxiety. When this happens, shift your focus and look for a trustworthy Source each moment. You don't have to agree with what transpired to find anything positive.

Not every moment of your life is ideal, but that doesn't mean it's all bad. Take the time to appreciate each moment and find something pleasant, no matter how small. Keep in mind that every encounter is an opportunity.

Recognize that you have little control over everything.

You may not agree with every change, but you cannot always prevent it. Accept changes without judgment or resistance. When you adjust to things as they happen Give up attempting to control things and allow life to take its course. You'll be more open to satisfying interactions along the way, which will help you enjoy the unavoidable changes.

Remember to accept without judging.

As a result, you should avoid judging the situation. Finding the source of a shift is not always easy, and attempting to do so can increase your anxiety. Accept and welcome change as you let go of the past.

Confidence in oneself

When Fear and concern take over, being self-assured will assist. Create an inner confidence that allows you to face your fears and take on complex activities.

If you have self-confidence and self-esteem, you will feel less apprehensive about the future because you will be confident that you made the proper decisions.

Chapter 3

How to kill your inner weakling

Taming Your Inner Critic: 7 Steps to Silencing It
Your inner conversation will propel you forward or hold you back from realizing your most significant potential.
Your inner conversation will propel you forward or hold you back from realizing your most significant potential.

Private dialogues with yourself can be a tremendous stepping stone or a massive impediment to accomplishing your goals. If your inner monologue says things like, "I'm going to embarrass myself," or "No one is going to talk to me," you're not come across as comfortable and friendly when you go into a cocktail party. Or, if you're thinking in the middle of an interview, "I'm never going to get this job," you'll struggle to present yourself confidently. Those pessimistic predictions can sometimes become a self-fulfilling prophecy.

Your thoughts strongly influence how you feel and behave, and negative self-talk can become dangerously self-destructive. Telling yourself that you'll never be successful or not as excellent as others will lower your self-esteem and prevent you from tackling your anxieties.

Thinking negatively
If you are overly critical of yourself, you are not alone. The majority of people struggle with self-doubt and harsh self-reflection. Fortunately, you do not have to endure verbal abuse. Instead, confront your negative thoughts and engage in a more fruitful dialogue with yourself. Here are seven techniques for taming your inner Critic:

1. Become conscious of your ideas. We become so accustomed to hearing our

narrations that it's easy to lose sight of the messages we're sending ourselves. Our perceptions are frequently inflated, discriminatory, and disproportionate. Pay attention to your thoughts and understand that just because you have an emotion does not mean it is accurate.

2. Quit ruminating. When you make a mistake or have a poor day, you may be tempted to repeatedly replay the events in your thoughts. However, constantly reminding yourself of that humiliating thing you did or that dubious thing you said will make you feel worse and not address the situation.

When you think rather than actively problem-solving, don't waste time reminding yourself, "Don't think about that." Instead, divert your attention to an activity, such as going for a walk, rearranging your desk, or chatting about something completely unrelated, and stop the critical thoughts before they spiral out of hand. The more you try not to think about something, the more you think about it.

3. Consider what counsel you would provide to a friend. If a friend showed self-doubt, you shouldn't say things like, "You can't ever do anything right," or "You're so stupid." "Everyone dislikes you." Yet we are frequently guilty of saying such things to ourselves. Instead, you'd be likelier to tell a friend, "You made a mistake, but it's not the end of the world," or "It's unlikely that today's performance will get you fired." Treat yourself like a friend, and use those words of encouragement.

4. Investigate the evidence. Recognize when your critical thoughts are excessively pessimistic. Examine the information that supports and refutes your prediction, "I'll never be able to quit my job and run my own business." things can be beneficial to write things down at times. Make a line down the

center of a piece of paper. List all of the evidence that supports your point of view on one side. On the other hand, list all the evidence to the contrary. Examining data from all sides of the debate can help you see the problem more rationally and less emotionally.

5. Replace highly critical statements with more accurate ones. Convert an unduly opposing viewpoint into more rational and realistic data. Replace the thought, "I never do anything right," with something more balanced, such as, "Sometimes I do things well, and sometimes I don't." Respond with a more accurate statement each time you have exaggeratedly negative thinking.

6. Consider the consequences if your suspicions were proven. It's easy to see a minor incident developing into a major disaster. However, the worst-case situation is frequently better than we think. For example, consider how horrible it would be

if you anticipated embarrassing yourself during a presentation.

Would you be able to recover if you embarrassed yourself, or do you believe it would kill your career? Reminding yourself that you can handle difficult situations or challenges boosts your confidence and reduces the constant barrage of worrying thoughts.

7. Strive for a balance of acceptance and self-improvement. There's a difference between constantly telling yourself you need to be better and reminding yourself that you can improve. Although it may appear to be counterintuitive, you can accomplish both. Accept your imperfections, but resign to working on the issues you want to fix.

You can admit that you have social anxiety while simultaneously deciding to grow more comfortable with public speaking. Accepting your flaws for what they are today does not obligate you to remain that way. Recognize your imperfections but resolve to stay a work in progress as you attempt to improve.

The Influence of Your Inner Dialogue
Your inner conversation will propel you forward or hold you back from realizing your most significant potential. While your inner CriticCritic can help you identify areas for improvement, overly harsh negative self-talk will degrade your performance and diminish your chances of reaching your goals. To coach yourself constructively and helpfully, practice taming your inner CriticCritic and silence the negativity.

How to Get Rid of Your Inner Critic
A wrong mental narrative can demoralize and sabotage you. These negative signals are known as your inner CriticCritic, and they significantly influence how you feel and behave, which can lead to damaging negative self-talk. Fortunately, there are techniques for turning negative thoughts into personal power and motivation sources.

What Exactly Is an Inner Critic?
The inner CriticCritic informs you why you need to be better. It is established due to difficult early childhood experiences in which we may have watched or experienced harsh attitudes toward ourselves or others close to us. As we mature, we unintentionally adopt and integrate this thought pattern toward ourselves and others.

The self-critical inner voice is tenacious in its judgment and criticism. This dynamic can result in mental health issues such as depression.3 The deluge of negative emotions and feelings associated with your inner CriticCritic can also be a significant source of stress and self-sabotage. Anxiety is another mental health ailment that can be linked to your inner Critic'sCritic's continual negative feedback.

Can an Inner Critic Be Beneficial?

The inner CriticCritic might be considered a survival system for detecting potential environmental hazards. It can also aid in the avoidance of failure or embarrassment. Furthermore, the inner critic can motivate people to improve and attain their goals. It can also inform you what you can do to improve matters.

The Inner Critic is a one-trick pony. It only understands how to blame, shame, or criticize itself. Our Inner Critic argues it is our FAULT when our needs are not met as children. We believe that the Inner Critic is looking out for our best interests and seeks to "improve" us and make us feel more sufficient. This is not true."

Examples of Inner Critics
The nurturing voice that coexists with the inner CriticCritic might be louder and crueler than the inner Critic'sCritic. Society can also repeat these signals, promoting the

notion that we are unique, unequal, or do not fit in with others.

Here are some instances of inner critical thinking:

You are unattractive.

You are overweight.

You are not deserving of this honor.

Nobody likes you, and nobody cares what you think or say.

You don't have any acquaintances.

You do not earn this position.

You are a forger.

The Effects of an Inner Critic

The inner critic can undermine self-esteem and your ability to trust yourself and your intuition, perpetuating a cycle of self-blame. It also allows for the growth of self-doubt. The toxicity of repeated negative self-thoughts can result in feelings of helplessness and hopelessness, as well as a decrease in motivation.

Continuous self-criticism can lead to emotional lows that lead to a mental health crisis such as depression or anxiety. Society also transmits negative signals about people's gender, race, or religion, which might be absorbed. These statements might make people feel unequal, mocked, or marginalized.

Inner critical voice experts warn that it can have much more severe repercussions, which exist on a severity scale. Suicidal people's thoughts have been found to shift from guilty self-accusations to destructive self-attacks to self-harm practices at some point.

How to Get Rid of Your Inner Critic
The inner critical voice does not go away, but there are measures you can take to train your inner voice to be compassionate and kind to yourself. You can attempt to remove yourself from the inner critical voice and reduce its power to deliver negative and

judgmental messages with greater self-awareness and direction. While the Inner Critic may be strong, it can be calmed by the voice of an Inner Coach," it is recommended.

 As the CriticCritic grows stronger over time, so can our Inner Coach. The CriticCritic may never totally vanish, but we can acquire techniques to decrease its destructive impact, and, as a result, we can establish new brain networks that support our well-being and self-esteem.We must train ourselves to handle discomfort by refraining from self-criticism, accepting positive feedback, and using supportive language with ourselves."

Here are eight steps to silence your critical inner voice:
1. Be Kind to Yourself
When the critical inner voice appears, take a step back. Show yourself the same compassion that you would provide to

others. Be understanding of your behavior, ideas, and feelings, including self-judgment and self-criticism.

2.   Think about Acceptance and Commitment Therapy (ACT).
Instead of attempting to change unpleasant ideas, ACT suggests observing and absorbing what our inner critic says before letting it go. Treat the inner CriticCritic as a mind-chatter and try to divert your focus away from it.6

3. Shift your perspective from being against yourself to being for yourself.
To begin, recognize the negative thoughts and beliefs you have. Try writing these thoughts in the second person, as if you were talking to someone else. Talk to a close friend who has a more positive view.

4. Investigate Cognitive Behavioral Therapy (CBT).

CBT is a brief therapy that offers ways to help change negative thinking about difficult situations and relationships. It gives people more control over their ideas and changes negative thinking into positive thinking, resulting in a healthier end.

5. Recognize When Your Inner Critic Appearance
Be proactive in identifying places, situations, events, and people that may cause your inner CriticCritic to arise. This will assist you in preparing for its onset. Then you can devise tactics to change these unfavorable behavioral habits.

6. Recognize that the inner CriticCritic will not go away.
Accept that we all have a constant internal conversation that influences our thoughts, behaviors, and actions. This is common and correct. You may, however, alter how you engage with and react to your inner Critic'sCritic's unfavorable aspects. Change

the relationship to be more of a friend than a foe.

7. Consider how your self-critical attitudes evolved within you.
To acquire more meaningful insights, try digging down the source of these harmful ideas. Who does it make you think of? Are there any underlying triggers or previous incidents causing these negative thoughts and self-talk? Step aside from the criticism to watch it; this will help you dis-identify from it and cease supporting it.

8. Use Humor as a Coping Strategy
Consider who you want to be the source of your inner critical voice. Consider your inner critic a cartoon or fictitious character from a film or television show. Select a character whose voice you find silly and who acts ineptly. With these features, it is much easier to reject an inner critic.

When Should You Consider Therapy?

If you can't quiet your inner CriticCritic, it's time to consider consulting a mental health expert. A therapist can provide insights, skills, and tactics to keep your inner CriticCritic in check and help you feel more in control when it appears. A mental health specialist can be found in the Choosing

Therapy directory.
 You're prepared to make a shift.
Your humiliation and pain are interfering with your pleasure and achievement.
You want more satisfying and helpful connections.
Another sign that counseling is needed is when anxiety and depression symptoms arise, persist, or worsen. Stress symptoms include:
Persistent anxiety that something horrible may happen.
A racing heart.
An inability to sleep or relax.

Last Words on the Inner Critic

We all have an inner critic who tells us terrible stories about ourselves. That voice can be louder, more frequent, and more annoying for some people.

Having a new sense of control over your critical inner voice can dramatically improve your quality of life. If you don't have a trusted friend or family member to turn to, counseling can significantly empower you.

Chapter 4

The skill to attract successfully

5 Ways to Increase Your Chances of Success
Take the quiz.
The way the universe works is frequently a mystery. The Law of Attraction works by empowering one's thoughts and manifestations. It's commonly said that everything you need appears when you need it. As a result, we should have more faith in the universe and less resistance to it. We can employ the Law of Attraction to attract what we want by intentionally changing our perspective. Here are five methods for attracting success into your life.

1. State Your Desires Clearly
To start actively attracting success, you must first define success for yourself. Take the time to put down the goals and desires you want to achieve. Make your goals as explicit as possible, as vague goals may lead to you

attracting alternate options. It would be helpful if you were specific about what you want to do when completing it and how you intend to accomplish it. Having your goals written down lets you focus on what you need to work on. To understand more about formulating and preparing your objectives, check out the 30X Life Program.

2. Become the person who achieves your objectives.

After you've written down your goals and ambitions, examine the type of person in charge of carrying them through. Do you need to improve your communication abilities? Do you want to broaden your business knowledge? Spending more time enhancing your leadership skills to run your organization better would be beneficial. You will also begin to attract individuals of the same type into your life. When you adopt a more positive and goal-oriented outlook, you'll notice more opportunities to interact with others who share your desire to become better versions of themselves.

3. Increase Your Confidence
It would be beneficial if you began to believe in the universe and your abilities to achieve your goals. You can only succeed if you dare to believe in yourself and constantly push yourself. Replace everything. It would be beneficial if you spent more time picturing your desired success. Please spend a few minutes meditating in the morning, pondering and showing your goals. Begin your day with positive affirmations. Positive affirmations will strengthen your positive energy, and you will begin to believe what you are saying to yourself.

4. Pay Close Attention to Positive Moments
Get your most excellent entrepreneurial characteristics immediately!
Take the quiz.
When opportunities present themselves, it is critical to express gratitude. When we

express gratitude, we repel lousy energy and bring more favorable opportunities into our lives. We can express our appreciation by appreciating the lovely things happening and returning the same point to the world by treating others with respect. Don't look for an excuse to complain if the opportunities provided to you aren't what you expected.

5. Accept the Positive Energy Around You
You are continually attracting positive energy by maintaining the appropriate vibe. Because positive energy attracts positive energy, you must keep an optimistic attitude toward life and your goals.
Make a good atmosphere for yourself by surrounding yourself with people who inspire and motivate you to achieve your goals. Looking for people or harmful behaviors that may generate problems in your life is critical.

When your perspective shifts, you will see that life is bountiful and everyone has access to various opportunities. You can recognize more fortunate opportunities if you use these five tactics.

Chapter 5

You approach and how to do it

The top eight approaches for approaching anyone, anywhere, and at any time
Get a relationship, nail an interview, meet mentors, and find a profession that will move you forward in business, love, and life if you master it. You were compelled to introduce yourself to someone new at least once this week, whether a beautiful girl on the street, a professional hero at a conference, or a guy at a cafe.

Who appeared to be a good buddy.
And you passed up at least one of those chances before opting not to jump.
Four Signs She Likes You
It's pretty standard. Connecting with a stranger gives up a new universe of exciting possibilities, such as trust and affirmation. However, it carries all the dreadful risks of discomfort, mistrust, and rejection. This has

a sound evolutionary explanation. Being outside your established tribe can be harmful (a relic of our archaic ancestors), whereas staying in your comfort zone protects your safety. Let's face it: other people can be scary.

Here are five methods to creating the ultimate social network before you need it:
However, conversing with a stranger can change your life. We've seen men overcome their fear of talking to strangers to land relationships, secure interviews, meet mentors, find employment opportunities, and build a solid social network. If you can control your nervousness and understand how and when to approach strangers, your life will swiftly open up in ways you never imagined.

Earn It!: How to Get a Raise Correctly?
So here are eight techniques to help you conquer your fear of approaching strangers and become a master of it.

Determine Possibilities

Take advantage of any opportunity to communicate with someone provided by the universe. That usually implies that you should accept it. Most failed attempts result from people needing additional chances to meet new people or ignoring them.

You'll notice someone engrossed in an excellent book as you stroll by. The characters are generally unnoticeable. There will be no apparent signals beckoning you in from the outside world, only fair chances for you to drop by and introduce yourself. In a pub, a girl may approach you too closely. A conference speaker will have some downtime.

So, take those! When you start seeing and seizing opportunities, you'll be surprised at how many there are. All excellent strategies flow from that first step.

Recognize Your Panic

We should not act as if approaching people is easy. Even after meeting tens of thousands of people, I still get that familiar flutter when I see someone I like. That genetic predisposition is firmly imprinted.

I won't encourage you to "conquer your fear" or "embrace the risk" since that would be like advising you to become more visible. Instead, admit that you are terrified and that there are dangers. It will considerably reduce the feeling of terror. What could go wrong? It is a lovely question to ask oneself to conquer worry. Our worst fears hardly ever come true. At the absolute least, you'll learn something about yourself and become more approachable.

Remember that innovative techniques aren't usually the product of absolute certainty. They are the outcome of honestly acknowledging your fear and being willing to say "hello" in the face of it. Fear is a sign

of being human, not of being weak. People also like socializing with one another.
Never be frightened to break social norms.
It would simply not be "proper" to approach someone. There will be terrible times ahead, such as when someone is on the phone or out with someone she likes.

However, what your mind usually calls "inappropriate" means "not served on a silver platter." The bulk of interesting people will want assistance in contacting them. Your goal should be to maturely flout cultural conventions rather than always to be precisely "acceptable."

Hello, lonesome man enjoying breakfast. Then make your way over to the girl drinking with her friends. Please request five minutes from the author. Be thoughtful, concise, and friendly. Worst-case scenario: People may think you're strange. Ideally, you put yourself in a position to begin a new relationship.

5 Stress and Anxiety Management Techniques

Make It Known That You Are Normal

This is the most practical advice I can give you about approaching. You must demonstrate your worth in a culture full of weirdos, psychopaths, and people who continually expect something from you (and believe me, most girls are conditioned to expect guys to fall into one of those categories).

As a result, approach your female drinking companion.

Every step you take exemplifies this. You approach with friendliness, gentleness, and patience.

With your open, confident body language. Your first line, "Hi, I'm sorry to bother you when you're enjoying breakfast, but you seem cool, so I wanted to say hello," indicates your pleasant disposition. These characteristics demonstrate that you are a stable, dependable, and consistent individual.

Every productive communication begins with the other person trusting you. Negative approaches, even from sound guys, are expected when the method's target suspects a hidden agenda or destructive intent. Remember that making a mistake is challenging as long as you appear safe and normal—even if your approach fails and you approach the female companion you're drinking with.

5 Steps to Self-Reinvention
Establish rapport and trust as soon as possible.
Similarly, developing rapport is one of the quickest ways to gain someone's trust. Contrary to common assumption, rapport-building does not entail attempting to find specific points of similarity with the other person. When a girl talks about her terrier, a guy who immediately recalls losing

his labrador usually appears overly ingratiating and self-centered. We emphasize the importance of finding a familiar experience on the first day of our residential program. "It sounds like you had a strong bond with your dog." When I received my tabby, I felt like my life had changed. Isn't it true that dogs and cats are the best?

As a result, approach your female drinking companion.
Finding commonalities is a beautiful way to build trust. If you hang around in the same circles, go to the same schools, or have similar hobbies, mentioning these things will imply that you belong to the same tribe. (Once again, consider man and evolution.) It's OK to advertise those, such as the Labrador story if you don't know anyone in common. Seek ways to build trust, especially early on, as this will pave the way for more excellent communication.

Making a Good First Impression
Only genuine compliments should be given. According to popular social dynamics theory, you should avoid complimenting others, especially females and young people. That is correct in many cases, but not because of the compliment. The complement's purpose is critical.

Consider why you feel the urge to compliment someone, whether it's your literary role model or the bartender. Are you looking to gain favor? How about a smooth entry? Or do you want to show the other person your admiration?

I frequently express my affection for folks I admire. If your compliment is genuine, you should be able to share it with anyone, even a stranger. And if you genuinely mean it, your compliments will come across as honest, considerate, and genuine rather than false or manipulative.

Why do my compliments fail to reach women?

Discover nonverbal communication.

When conversing with strangers, you must be proficient at reading nonverbal cues. It would be beneficial if you began learning about body language and verbal subtext.

The most intriguing things should often be said. When a woman in a bar turns to face you and continues the conversation, she tells you you are welcome. If she doesn't make eye contact and instead turns to face her group, it's time to move on. Like the recruiting manager who checks his email, the manager who chooses to hang out with you is investing time in getting to know you.

These indications are typically less pronounced:

A quick glimpse.

A lengthy handshake. This is a well-thought-out follow-up inquiry.

A willingness to drop a book and engage in conversation.

People will usually tell you whether their vibe fits yours. Consider these clues and use them to adjust your methods. It is your responsibility to pay attention and respond accordingly.
Recognizing Her Body Language

Take Initiative
Any effective strategy will include a plan for connecting later. Regardless of how well you perform in your first meeting, you must follow up in some way, whether by phone, text, email, or social media.

There is no secret recipe here. All you have to do is pledge to follow through. Although it may appear simple, you'd be shocked how many men need to follow through. They meet with a potential employer in person but have yet to set up a phone conversation to discuss the opportunity. They meet a cute girl but don't say anything to her for several days or weeks. It is, indeed, without justification. If you're going to approach, do it entirely and continue to advance your connection.

If not, you will not benefit from taking a chance and approaching a stranger.

Chapter 6

Learning to make better decision
Why is it critical to make intelligent decisions?

Ten Rules for Making Sound Decisions
Sometimes all that is required is picking what shoes to wear to work. (This can be challenging with a commute and other events during the day.)

However, when critical circumstances necessitate quick action, it can be challenging to make sensible decisions without a technique to assist you.

Let's look at how to make better decisions and create habits to make the process easier.

Why is it critical to make intelligent decisions?
Individual choices may not be necessary in the here and now.

In general, the outcomes of such decisions impact how your life turns out. Better judgments result in better outcomes (and fewer consequences). Making smarter choices may present you with more options and freedom. A good choice, on the other hand, can exclude particular possibilities while opening up new ones.

Making better choices also implies that you are learning from your mistakes in the past. Learning from your mistakes is also an essential part of personal development.
Making sound decisions is critical for achieving a healthy work-life balance in your personal life. Making wise judgments may improve your career and personal happiness. As a result, you may progress professionally and generate superior work.

Making decisions will eventually define you as a workplace leader.
group-of-employees-having-a-conversation-how-to-make-better-decisions

You must be determined if you wish to lead. Furthermore, as a leader, your actions will have an impact on others as well as oneself. As a result, it's critical to consider all of the variables and probable repercussions of a decision.

Making decisions like a multibillion-dollar corporation necessitates establishing the backdrop and examining the options.
Three methods to assist you in making better selections

Do you want to discover how to make essential decisions correctly?
These three habits can assist you in making more informed decisions in your personal and professional life.

1. Allow yourself time to reflect on your mistakes (and triumphs).
It would be beneficial if you gave them some thought to learn from your blunders. As a result, it would be helpful if you made it a

practice to schedule frequent periods of introspection in your calendar. This may benefit your mental health as well.

This isn't just for you to dwell on your mistakes or berate yourself for making bad decisions. Use it as a timed opportunity to reflect on your day's choices objectively and examine why some were better (or worse) than others.

Consider why you made the mistakes that you did. Your assumption needed to be modified, or else you would have yet to receive additional advice.

Perhaps you acted without giving yourself time to consider or because you were afraid. Examine the problem from every viewpoint and think about any other possibilities you have had. What did you learn? What will you do differently tomorrow as a result?
You will need help to correct your mistakes. However, you can train yourself to take

advice from those decisions to become a better decision-maker.

2. Examine your level of certainty.
Exuding confidence is essential, especially when taking on new job-related responsibilities.
Overconfidence, on the other hand, may impair your ability to make decisions. In medicine, overconfidence can lead to diagnostic errors.

Are you sure you understand what you're doing? If this is the case, you may have an overconfidence condition. Make it a habit to review yourself regularly to keep your overconfidence under check.

Be mindful of the unknown. We can admit how little we know or have control over while remaining steadfast in our decision. It will ensure that you continue seeking alternate perspectives and weighing different solutions.

If you feel overconfident, seek other people's perspectives to acquire a new viewpoint.

confident-woman-with-headphones-how-to-make-better-decisions. Even if you believe you can always be correct, you will not be. Conversely, if you notice a lack of confidence, address it. Consider establishing more realistic trust. This is especially important if you suffer from impostor syndrome.

3. Identify your mental shortcuts.
People use heuristics, or mental shortcuts, to make quick judgments.
Heuristics can be helpful since they reduce the thought necessary to make judgments.

Handling your difficulties for you, lowering the complexity of issues, and assisting you in making a decision more swiftly
Heuristics, on the other hand, can lead to cognitive biases.

One example is the availability heuristic. It is more likely to decide based on facts that come to mind promptly.

As a result, if you've recently read several news articles on poisonous managers, you're more likely to spot toxic behavior in the leaders around you.

It's critical to understand the heuristics you use as a result. These heuristics may influence how you make judgments daily.

While our heuristics feel comfortable and natural, implementing them involves some effort. They appeared to be realistic. Knowing what they are allows you to take a breather and analyze how they affect your decisions.

Take a step back and consider what other possibilities have been available that you still need to choose or explore. What would have occurred if things had gone differently? When the time comes, this will help you determine whether or not your heuristics are supporting you in making better decisions.

Make it a habit to be conscious of your assumptions and to consider the grounds for your beliefs and judgments.
woman-standing-with-hands-crossed-how-to-make-better-decisions.

Ten Rules for Making Sound Decisions
Making sound decisions necessitates the development of good habits. So, what can you do when facing a difficult decision?
Here are some decision-making recommendations to help you make better decisions more quickly:

1. Imagine yourself a year from today.
When you're forced to make a decision you're unsure about, try envisioning the future. Make a plan for the coming year and the next five years. It's critical to avoid focusing solely on the immediate consequences of your decisions.

The results you see immediately may only occasionally indicate whether or not you made the proper decision. Consider all potential variables. Think about one option and how it will affect your future. Then, compare your choice to others.

What do you want to achieve in a year? After five years? And how do these numerous options affect your objectives?

Although this one-year gap should not be your deciding factor, considering it can help you think about how the current conditions work to your advantage.

Consider the scenario before considering whether to accept a new employment offer or keep your current one.
Consider your current position's prospective future. Compare that to what the new deal can do for you in a year. Which one best meets your requirements?

2. Make a list of your goals.

The previous one-year exercise may be helpful when making big decisions.

However, it is only accurate if you know where you want to travel in a year. How would you know which decisions are bad and which will get you closer to your goals if you don't?

As a result, you must set aside some time to sit down and create your goals and a personal vision statement that compliments them. These goals must be both personal and professional.
woman
-taking-notes-on-a-laptop-computer-how-to
-make-better-decisions

Let's go back to the previous example of a new job offer. If one of your goals is to become a leader at work, writing them down will help you assess which path will bring you closer to them in a year.

You know you'd be better off staying in your current position if the new job offer pays you more but gives you fewer opportunities to build your leadership skills.

3. Provide at least four alternatives.
Consider at least four before deciding unless you must choose between two possibilities. Even if you assume there are only two possibilities, try to think imaginatively and examine all of them. The more options you know, the better informed your decision will be.

On the other hand, if you explore two options, you can overlook one that helped you get closer to your goal. Consider the following scenario: you must determine which side of a disagreement between two coworkers to trust. Nonetheless, there are some different opinions on this subject.

You could look for other witnesses to the argument who were present before you. As a result, you may develop a story based on more than one person's testimony. A compromise-based conclusion is possible.

4. Recognize your need for more knowledge. Any decision you make will almost certainly entail unknown situations. But you are entirely ignorant of your ignorance. That is why spending a moment looking for those strange things is critical. Once you've identified what you don't know, you can take the measures necessary to learn more.

The more you know, the better your chances of making an informed decision based on all the facts. Assume you're still examining your two previous job alternatives. You must be aware of the leadership chances available in your new employment. This data informs you which decisions will bring you closer to your objectives. You can inquire about leadership chances with a friend who works there.

5. Remove yourself from the situation.
It's difficult to see all the facts when you're in the thick of an issue.

Remove yourself from the situation you're trying to decide on. Use the distance to complete the preceding phases, such as brainstorming alternate ideas or visualizing yourself a year from now.

For example, you may need to form a team for a complex project at work. You're stuck in your office, attempting to find the best candidates for the job. Take a step back and alter your perspective. A change of location might provide you with the view you need to make better decisions.

6. Own up to your faults
It takes effort to confront your faults. However, doing so can help you make better selections in the future.
Consider similar scenarios in which you may have made a mistake when making your

decision. Determine what actions you took or did not do that contributed to your error.

In the last case, you could have assembled a poorly performing team. You understand that you let your friendship with a team member affect your decisions by facing your faults. You are now aware of your biases. You can make new decisions while keeping your prejudices in mind.

7. Seek feedback.
Receiving input from others helps broaden your perspective. It can help you eliminate your prejudices and reveal previously unknown options.

Using the team-building example, ask someone you can trust for their perspective on your potential team ideas. Someone else may notice a team flaw you would not have seen otherwise.

8. Consider both the short-term and long-term consequences.
While looking ahead a year is a valuable exercise, examining the immediate and long-term consequences of a decision is essential. How will this decision influence your life in a week?

What will occur in a month? What if it was three, five, or ten years?
For example, you know that relocating across the country will significantly impact your life. In the short term, your life will be influenced as well. List the short and long-term consequences of staying or leaving.

9. Examine data
Following your instincts may put you in danger at times. Discover some unbiased data points to round out your understanding of the scenario. For example, look into employment availability, crime rates, and cost of living statistics if you're considering

relocating nationwide. If you move with the help of these data points, you will have a better grasp of your future.

10. Recognize and uphold your principles.
This is critical. Your values guide and set boundaries, especially when making decisions in a fast-changing or unpredictable world.

Goals are essential, but so are personal and professional values. Some believe having a separate vision statement keeps their values and actions in sync. Those who feel meaning and purpose in their work hold senior and skilled positions. Let's decide between your current position and the new offer.

If you appreciate inclusive leadership but your current employment functions differently, accepting a new offer from a more inclusive organization may be a good idea.

Learn how to make better decisions.
Coaching, in addition to these tips, may help you improve your decision-making talents. Avoiding decision fatigue, making better and faster judgments, and having confidence in your choices are possible.

Chapter 7

Secrets to being an irresistible catch

8 Essential Techniques for Increasing
Attractiveness and Irresistibility
You can't help but admire them.
Enjoyable people are always around certain
people, attracting the most attractive girls or
guys. You're still single and looking for "the
one" now.

Have you spent your entire life seeking that
one "special" person? Someone fantastic will
appear, solve your problems, and make the
world right for you.

What about some people that attract others,
like bees, to honey?
What do they have that you don't?
Very appealing and a great catch
You can't help but admire them.

Enjoyable people are always around certain people, attracting the most attractive girls or guys.
You're still single and looking for "the one" now.

Have you spent your entire life seeking that one "special" person? Someone fantastic will appear, solve your problems, and make the world right for you.

What about some people that attract others, like bees, to honey?

What do they have that you don't?
Are they employing any dubious mental tricks? Or do they exude a magnetic personality?
I used to be just as curious.

I even joined a dubious covert seduction group a few years ago, where I got to hang out with numerous guys who taught me all kinds of sneaky ways to influence and trick women into liking me.

That didn't last long; it felt sneaky, repulsive, and unpredictable.

Suddenly, I realized that the most important was who I was and how I presented myself to the world.
Take a look at this. Why would someone choose to be with you in the first place?
Being irresistible is inside work!
Then it hit me: I was the beginning point.

I assessed my life, discovered new hobbies and interests, and focused on becoming the best version of myself.
People started wanting to hang out with me out of nowhere. I made many new friends and even went on hot dates with females I had previously dismissed as out of my league.
I also started to become quite gorgeous and appealing.

1. Make others feel valuable and special.
The secret is to be genuinely interested in others.
This will result in a more powerful personal bond between you and everyone you meet. You automatically become more intriguing when you care about other people and are pulled to their tales.

Being honest with them, showing interest in their life, and learning about their interests facilitates the flow of conversation and forming a personal connection.

So, rather than being intriguing, be interested. If you make people feel special, they will perceive you as remarkable.
2. Strive to be the greatest that you can be.
You have a life vision and work daily to become your best version.
Follow a path of monetary and personal advancement since your inner development

comes first, followed by your outside product.

And learning to love and accept yourself for who you are, flaws and all, is a significant part of inner growth. Finding the right companion is how you can appreciate a flawed person, not how you fall in love.

3. Be considerate and kind to others.
Treat others how you want to be treated because how you treat those around you reveals much about who you are.
Learn to be kind and courteous to everyone who contributes to your everyday comfort and ease, such as waiters/waitresses, store clerks, etc.

Always be pleasant, respectful, and courteous to those you care about and closest to you, especially your family.
Reflect honestly on how you currently treat others and take action to change your behavior because how you treat others will

eventually define how you treat your future relationship.

4. Live Intentionally
If you live a meaningful and purposeful life, you will become much more intriguing and alluring. Knowing what matters to you and pursuing it will set you apart.

If you've been in a committed relationship for a time, a common life purpose, something significant and profound to you both, will keep you together through thick and thin. Aim to live a life of love and compassion if your mission is unknown.

5. Be Specific About Your Relationship Objectives.
Be explicit about what you want from a relationship and a potential spouse; the more detailed you are, the easier it will be to meet someone. While having a wish list for your companion is beneficial, look beyond their exterior looks. Examine prior

relationships to see what worked and what didn't.

Choose persons who can act as role models for you and investigate their relationships.

Engage in some people-watching since observing how couples communicate may teach you a lot.

6. Maintain Excellent Self-Care

Take the best possible care of yourself by examining your nutrition, developing an exercise plan, and maintaining regular medical exams. If you're in good health, you'll look better and have more energy for fun activities with your potential partner.

Rather than going crazy, focus on being moderately active and healthy. Adopt a simple, long-term improvement strategy; even a tiny amount each day will add up.

Examine your appearance, including your clothing, hairstyle, and cleanliness.

7. Maintain Clutter and Order in Your Future Love-Nest Declutter your home to

make it a nice, comfortable place for your prospective partner to visit.

Declutter your life and your home. You will get something unintentionally as well.

Please review my 20 questions now, as they will drastically simplify your life.

There is no time to spare; take action on every question you answer. "YES"!

Remember: Why would a specific person choose a slob?

8. Live a Happy Life and Follow Your Dreams

Make a fun life for yourself so someone else can contribute one day.

Be passionate about your life and your activities. Pursue your interests, whether they are sports, hiking, or activities such as salsa.

Start living before you meet your special someone; engage in activities alone or with others. Begin right away!

This boosts your chances of meeting someone special on such occasions.

11 Irresistible People's Secrets
Some people exude enthusiasm and confidence regardless of their lack of money, appearance, or social connections. Even the most cynical people are won over by these endearing characteristics. These people are the life and soul of every celebration. You turn to them for assistance, advice, and company.

You can't get enough of them and wonder, "What do they have that I don't?" "What makes them so appealing?"
What is the distinction? Their sense of self-worth is internal.

Irresistible people aren't continually seeking validation because they're self-assured enough to find it. Every day, they practice particular routines to keep this positive outlook.

Because being irresistible isn't a product of dumb chance, it's essential to study the patterns of appealing individuals so you can exploit them. Prepare to say "hello" to a more irresistible self.

1. They treat everyone with dignity.

Irresistible people are always friendly and respectful, whether engaging with their biggest customer or a server taking their drink order. They understand that no matter how pleasant they are to the person they're having lunch with if that person watches them misbehave toward someone else, it's all for none. Irresistible people treat everyone respectfully because they believe they are no better than anyone else.

2. They adhere to the Platinum Rule

The Golden Rule, which states that you should treat people as you would like to be treated, has a fatal flaw: it implies that everyone wants to be treated the same way. It ignores that a wide range of factors drives humans. One person enjoys being the center of attention, while another despises it. Irresistible people read other people well and alter their conduct and style to make others feel at ease. The Platinum Rule (treat people as you would like to be treated) corrects this issue.

3. They Avoid Small Talk

Small chat is the most effective strategy to avoid an emotional connection from establishing during a conversation. Even in short, daily discussions, irresistible individuals build bonds and find depth. Their genuine interest in other people allows them to ask practical questions and relate what they learn to several vital aspects of the speaker's life. Approaching people robotically with small talk puts their brains on autopilot and inhibits them from feeling natural affection for you.

4. They prioritize people over everything else.

Irresistible people genuinely care about others around them. They don't worry about how well they're loved since they're too preoccupied with the people they're with. As a result, they devote little time to self-reflection. It's what makes their irresistibility appear so natural.

To put this practice to use, try putting down your smartphone and focusing on the people around you. Concentrate on what they're saying rather than your reaction or how what they're saying will influence you.

When someone tells you something about themselves, ask open-ended inquiries to elicit even more information.

5. They don't overdo it.

Irresistible people do not dominate conversations with tales of their intelligence and achievement. They're not resisting the desire to boast. They don't even consider it since they know how unlikeable people who strive too hard to make others like them are.

6. They Understand the Distinction Between Fact and Opinion

Irresistible people tackle contentious and sensitive matters with grace and charm. When it comes to global warming, politics, vaccine schedules, or GMO foods, smart people know that many individuals are just as intelligent as they are but see things differently. They don't shy away from expressing their thoughts, but they make it clear that they are opinions, not facts.

7. They Are Genuine

Irresistible people are who they are. Nobody has to expend energy or brainpower guessing their agenda or predicting what they'll do next. They do this because they understand that no one appreciates a phony. People draw toward genuine people because they know they can rely on them. When you don't know who someone is or how they feel, it's simple to resist them.

They are trustworthy.
Integrity is a simple notion, yet it takes work to implement. People with great integrity are enticing because they speak plainly. To show integrity daily, motivate individuals to follow through, avoid gossiping about others, and do the right thing even when it hurts.

They Smiling
People naturally (and unconsciously) reflect the body language of the person they are conversing with. Smile at people during chats if you want them to find you irresistible; they will automatically return the favor and feel fabulous.

10. They Make An Effort To Look Good
There is a massive distinction between being presentable and being egotistical. Irresistible people recognize that trying to

appear your best is akin to cleaning your house before guests arrive—a sign of respect for others. They stop thinking about it after they've made themselves acceptable.

11. They Find Reasons to Appreciate Life
Positive and passionate people are irresistible. They are never bored because they view life as a fascinating adventure in which others want to participate.

Irresistible people have issues, even major ones, but they see them as transient roadblocks rather than unavoidable destinies. When things go wrong, they remind themselves that it is only one day and hope that the next day, week, or month will improve.

Putting It All Together
Irresistible people did not have fairy godmothers hovering over their cribs. They've honed some endearing characteristics and practices that everyone can embrace as their own.

They are more concerned with others than themselves, making others feel liked, respected, understood, and seen. Remember, the more you concentrate on others, the more irresistible you will become.